THE BUSHCRAFT HANDBOOKS

BUSH ROPEMAKING

Illustrations by the Author

Richard H. Graves

The Bushcraft Handbooks

Bush Ropemaking

Copyright © 1952 by Richard Graves
This Edition Copyright © 2013 by Palmer River Publishing

Cover, Graphics and Layout by: Palmer River Publishing

ISBN-13: 978-1484803073
ISBN-10: 1484803078

About The Author

The author of "The Bushcraft Handbooks", Richard Graves, is a member of the Irish literary family of that name. A veteran of the Great War campaigns in the Dardenelles and the Western Front, the author became passionate about the bush at an early age. As an enthusiastic bushwalker, skier and pioneer of white-water canoeing, he foresaw how a knowledge of bushcraft could save lives in the Second World War. To achieve this end, he initiated and led the Australian Jungle Rescue Detachment, assigned to the Far East American Air Force. This detachment of 60 specially selected A.I.F. soldiers successfully effected more than 300 rescue missions, most of which were in enemy-held territory in New Guinea, without failure of a mission or loss of a man.

An essential preliminary for rescue was survival, and it was for this purpose that the notes for these books were written. These notes were later revised and prepared for a School in Bushcraft which has been operating for several years and continues to provide valuable instruction to Servicemen embarking overseas on active service in Korea and Malaya.

Bushcraft

As far as is known, "The Bushcraft Handbooks" are unique. There is nothing quite like them, nor is any collection of published bushcraft knowledge as comprehensive.

The term "Bushcraft" is used because "woodcraft" commonly means either knowledge of local fauna and flora or else is associated with the blood-sports of hunting and shooting. "The Bushcraft Handbooks" include a volume on traps and snares, but these are purposely-designed to be completely ineffective for native animals which are insect enters or grazers. These traps have been included because they would only be effective in catching predatory animals such as cats and dogs which have taken to the bush, and other "pest" creatures such as feral swine or goat.

"Bushcraft" describes the activity of how to make use of natural materials found locally in any area. It includes many of the skills used by primitive man, and to these are added "white man" skills necessary for survival, such as time and direction, and the provision of modern "white man" comforts as illustrated in the volume on bush campcraft.

The practice of bushcraft develops in an individual a remarkable ability to adapt quickly to a changing environment. Because this is so, the activity is a valuable counter to the over-specialisation so prevalent in today's society, and is particularly significant in youth training and character-moulding work.

INTRODUCTION
to the BUSHCRAFT HANDBOOKS

THE PRACTICE OF BUSHCRAFT shows many unexpected results. The five senses are sharpened, and consequently the joy of being alive is greater. The individual's ability to adapt and improvise is developed to a remarkable degree. This in turn leads to increased self-confidence.

Self-confidence, and the ability to adapt to a changing environment and to overcome difficulties, is followed by a rapid improvement in the individual's daily work. This in turn leads to advancement and promotion.

Bushcraft, by developing adaptability, provides a broadening influence, a necessary counter to offset the narrowing influence of modern specialisation.

For this work of bushcraft all that is needed is a sharp cutting implement: knife, axe or machete. The last is the most useful. For the work, dead materials are most suitable. The practice of bushcraft conserves, and does not destroy, wild life.

R.H.G.
April, 1952

CONTENTS

BUSH ROPEMAKING

One of the first needs in Bushcraft is the ability to join poles or sticks. The only method available is by the use of lashings.

To use lashings however, it is necessary to have, find or make, ropes or cordage for this purpose.

The ability to spin, or plait fibres into ropes or cords is one of the oldest of man's primitive skills. The method is simple, and follows precisely the same stages that are made use of by today's complicated machines.

The material from which to spin or plait ropes or cords is in abundance everywhere. Any fibrous material which has reasonable length, moderate strength and is flexible or pliable can be used. These are the three things to look for, and they can be found in many vines, grasses, barks, palms, and even in the hair of animals.

The breaking strains of handmade ropes and cords varies greatly with different materials, consequently it is essential that the rope or cord be tested for the purpose for which it will be used, before being actually put to use.

The uses to which these hand-made ropes and cords can be put, apart from lashing, is almost endless, and some few are included in this book.

The Making of Ropes and Cords

Almost any natural fibrous material can be spun into good serviceable rope or cord, and many materials which have a length of 12 to 24 inches, or more can be braided or plaited. Ropes of up to 3 and 4 inches diameter can be 'laid' by four people, and breaking strains for bush-made rope of one inch diameter range from 100 lbs. to as high as 2,000 or 3,000 lbs.

Breaking Strains

Taking a three lay rope of 1 inch diameter as standard, the following table of breaking strains may serve to give a fair idea of general strengths of various materials. For safety sake always regard the lowest figure as the breaking strain unless you know otherwise.

Green Grass	100 lbs. to 250 lbs.
Bark Fibre	500 lbs. to 1,500 lbs.
Palm Fibre	650 lbs. to 2,000 lbs.
Sedges	2,000 lbs. to 2,500 lbs.
Monkey Rope (Lianas) ..	560 lbs. to 700 lbs.
Lawyer Vine (Calamus) ..	½ inch dia. 1,200 lbs.

Double the diameter quadruples the breaking strain.

Halve the diameter, and you reduce the breaking strain to one fourth.

Principles of Bush Ropemaking

To discover whether a material is suitable for rope making it must have four qualities:

1. It must be reasonably long in the fibre.
2. It must have 'strength.'
3. It must be pliable.
4. And it must have 'grip' so that the fibres will 'bite' onto one another.

GRASS BARK LENGTH   TWIST   PLIABLE

There are three simple tests to find if any material is suitable.

First pull on a length of the material to test it for strength. The second test, to be applied if it has strength, is to twist it between the fingers and 'roll' the fibres together; if it will stand this and not 'snap' apart, tie a thumb knot in it, and gently tighten the knot. If the material does not cut upon itself, but allows the knot to be pulled taut, then it is suitable for rope making, providing that the material will 'bite' together and is not smooth or slippery.

You will find these qualities in all sorts of plants, in ground vines, in most of the longer grasses, in some of the water reeds and rushes, in the inner barks of many trees and shrubs, and in the long hair or wool of many animals.

Some green freshly gathered materials may be 'stiff' or unyielding. When this is the case try passing it through hot flames for a few moments. The heat treatment should cause the sap to burst through some of the cell structure, and the material thus becomes pliable.

Fibres for rope making may be obtained from many sources:

Surface roots of many shrubs and trees have strong fibrous bark;
Dead inner bark of fallen branches of some species of trees and in the new growth of many trees such as willows;
In the fibrous material of many water and swamp growing plants and rushes;
In many species of grass and in many weeds;
In some sea weeds;
In fibrous material from leaves, stalks and trunks of many palms;
In many fibrous-leaved plants such as the aloes.

Gathering and Preparation of Materials

In some plants there may be a high content of vegetable gum and this can often be removed by soaking in water, or by boiling, or again, by drying the material and 'teasing' it into thin strips.

Some of the materials have to be used green it any strength is required. The materials that should be green include the sedges, water rushes, grasses, and lianas.

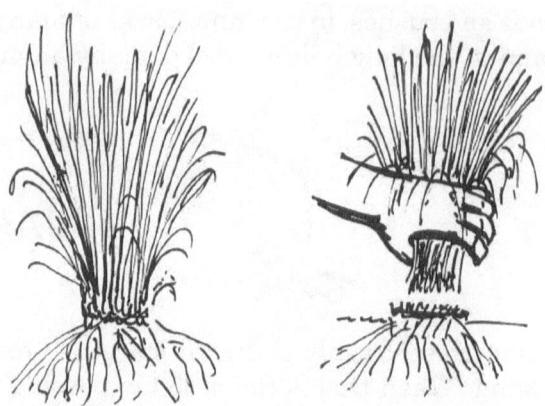

Grasses, sedges and water rushes should be cut and never pulled. *Cutting above ground level is 'harvesting,' but pulling up the plant means its 'destruction.'*

It is advisable not to denude an area entirely but to work over a wide location and harvest the most suitable material, leaving some for seeding and further growth.

For the gathering of sedges and grasses, be particularly careful therefore to 'harvest' the material, that is, cut what you require above ground level, and take only from the biggest clumps.

By doing this you are not destroying the plant, but rather aiding the natural growth, since your harvesting is truly pruning.

You will find that from a practical point of view this is far the easiest method.

Many of the strong-leafed plants are deeply rooted, and you simply cannot pull a leaf off them.

Palm fibre in tropical or sub-tropical regions is harvested. You will find it at the junction of the leaf and the palm trunk, or you will find it lying on the ground beneath many palms. Palm fibre is a 'natural' for making ropes and cords.

Fibrous matter from the inner bark of trees and shrubs is generally more easily used if the plant is dead or half dead. Much of the natural gum will have dried out and when the material is being teased, prior to spinning, the gum or resin will fall out in fine powder.

There may be occasions when you will have to use the bark of green shrubs, but avoid this unless it is absolutely essential, and only cut a branch here and there. *Never ever cut a complete tree just because you want the bark for a length of cord.*

To Make Cord by Spinning With the Fingers

Use any material with long strong threads or fibres which you have previously tested for strength and pliability. Gather the fibres into loosely held strands of even thickness. Each of these strands is twisted clockwise. The twist will hold the fibre together. The strands should be from 1/8" downwards–for a rough and ready rule there should be about 15 to 20 fibres to a strand. Two, three or four of these strands are later twisted together, and this twisting together or 'laying' is done with an anti-clockwise twist, while at the same time the separate strands which have not yet been laid up are twisted clockwise. *Each strand must be of equal twist and thickness.*

This illustration shows the general direction of twist and the method whereby the fibres are bonded into

strands. In similar manner the twisted strands are put together into lays, and the lays into ropes. Illustrated in this diagram is a two strand lay.

The person who twists the strands together is called the 'layer,' and he must see that the twisting is even, that the strands are uniform, and that the tension on each strand is equal. In laying, he must watch that each of the strands is evenly 'laid up,' that is, that one strand does not twist around the other two. (A thing you will find happening the first time you try to 'lay up.')

When spinning fine cords for fishing lines, snares, etc., considerable care must be taken to keep the strands uniform and the lay even. Fine thin cords of no more than one-thirty-second of an inch thickness can be spun with the fingers and they are capable of taking a breaking strain of twenty to thirty lbs. or more.

Normally two or more people are required to spin and lay up the strands for cord.

Many native people when spinning cord do so unaided, twisting the material by running the flat of the hand along the thigh, with the fibrous material between hand and thigh and with the free hand they feed in fibre for the next 'spin.' By this means one person can make long lengths of single stands.

This' method of making cord or rope with the fingers is slow if any considerable length of cord is required.

A more simple and easy way to rapidly make lengths of rope of fifty to a hundred yards or more in length is to make a rope-walk and set up multiple spinners in the form of cranks. The series of photographic illustrations on the succeeding pages show the details of rope spinning.

In a rope walk, each feeder holds the material under one arm and with one free hand feeds it into the strand which is being spun by the crank. The other hand lightly holds the fibres together till they are spun. As the lightly spun strands are increased in length they must be supported on cross bars. Do not let them lie on the ground. You can spin strands of twenty to one hundred yards before laying up. Do not spin the material in too thickly. Thick strands do not help strength in any way, rather they tend to make a weaker rope.

Layout of a rope walk.

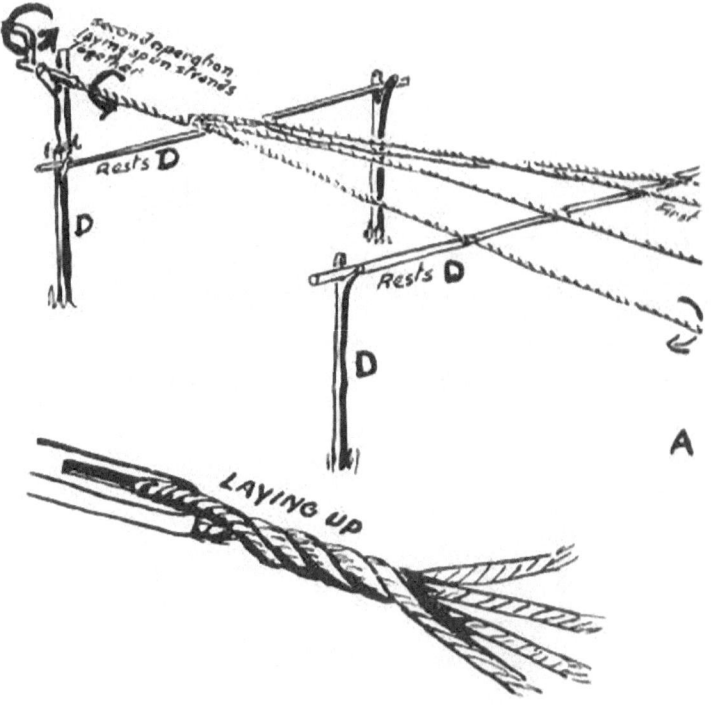

Setting up a Ropewalk

When spinning ropes of ten yards or longer it is necessary to set cross bars every two or three yards to carry the strands as they are spun. If cross bars are not set up the strands or rope will sag to the ground, and some of the fibres will tangle up with grass, twigs or dirt on the ground. Also the twisting of the free end may either be stopped or interrupted and the strand will be unevenly twisted.

The easiest way to set up crossbars for the rope walk is to drive pairs of forked stakes into the ground about six feet apart and at intervals of about six to ten feet. The cross bars must be smooth, and free from twigs and loose portions of bark that might twist in with the spinning strands.

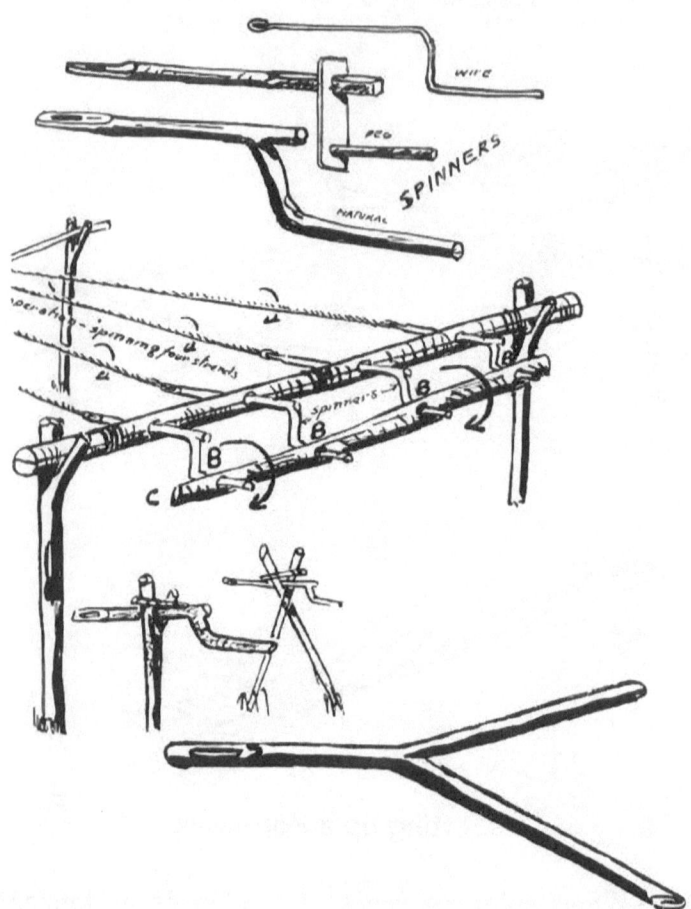

The cross bar A is supported by two uprights, and pierced to take the cranks B. These cranks can be made out of natural sticks, morticed slab, and pegs, or if available, bent wire. The connecting rod C enables one man to turn all cranks clockwise simultaneously. Crossbars supporting the strands as they are spun are shown D. A similar crank handle to C is supported on a fork stick at the end of the rope walk. This handle is turned in reverse (anti-clockwise) to the cranks C to twist the connected strands together. These are 'laid up' by one or more of the feeders.

Always make it a rule to turn the first strand clockwise, then the laying up of the strands will be done anti-clockwise and the next laying will again be clockwise.

Bark fibre being spun into strands using a single crank handle.

Spinner-feeder on right with bundle of material under his right arm feeds in material.

Joining the strands prior to lay up.

Testing the rope of bark fibre, breaking strain 1" diameter, about 800 lbs.

Close up of the finished rope.

Proof that your rope is well made will be if the individual fibres lie lengthways along the rope.

In the process of laying up the strands, the actual twisting together, or laying will take some of the original 'twist' out of the strand which has not yet been laid. Therefore it is necessary to keep twisting the strands whilst laying together.

When making a rope, too long to be spun and laid in one piece, a section is laid up, and coiled on the ground at the end of the rope walk farthest from the cranks. Strands for a second length are spun, and these strands are married or spliced into the strands of the first section and then the laying up of the second section continues the rope.

The actual 'marrying' of the strands is done only in the last lay, which when completed makes the rope. The ends where the strands are married should be staggered in different places. By this means rope can be made and extended in sections to a great length.

After your complete length of rope is laid up, pass it through fire, to burn off the loose ends and fibres. This will make your rope smooth and most, professional looking.

Laying the Strands

BAD LAYING | GOOD LAYING

The strands lie on these crossbars as they are spun. When the strands have been spun to the required length, which should be no more than about a hundred feet, they are joined together by being held at the far end. They are then ready for laying together.

The turner, who is facing the cranks, twists the ends together anti-clockwise, at the same time keeping his full weight on the rope and which is being layed up. The layer advances placing the strands side by side as they turn.

Laying up is very fast when the layer is experienced. He quickly gets the feeling of the work.

It is important to learn to feed the material evenly, and lay up slowly, thereby getting a smooth even rope. Do not try to rush the ropemaking. If you do you will have uneven, badly spun strands, and ugly lays, and poor rope. Speed in ropemaking only comes with practice. At first it will take a team of three or four up to two hours or more to make a 50-yard length of rope of three lays, each of three strands, that is nine strands for a rope with a finished diameter of about 1 inch. With practice the same three or four people will make the same rope in 15 to 20 minutes. These times do not include time for gathering material.

In feeding, the free ends of the strands twist in the loose material fed in by the feeder. The feeder must move backwards at a speed governed by the rate at which he feeds. As the feeder moves backwards he must keep a slight tension on the strands.

Making Rope with Single Spinner

Two people can make rope, using a single crank.

A portion of the material is fastened to the eye of the crank, as with the multiple crank, and the feeder holding the free ends of this strand against the bundle of loose material under his arm feeds in, walking backwards. Supporting crossbars, as used in a ropewalk, are required when a length of more than 20 or 30 feet is being spun.

Feeding

If the feeder is holding material under his left arm, his right hand is engaged in continuously pulling material forward to his left hand which feeds it into the turning strand. These actions done together as the feeder walks backwards govern the thickness of the strands. His left hand, lightly closed over the loose turning material, must 'feel' the fibres 'biting' or twisting together.

When the free end of the turning strand, which is against the loose material under his arm takes in too thick a tuft of the material he closes his left hand, and so arrests the twist of the material between his left hand and his bundle. This allows him to tease out the overfull 'bite,' with his right hand, and so he maintains a uniform thickness of the spinning strand. There is a knack in 'feeding' and once you have mastered this knack you can move backwards, and feed with considerable speed.

Thickness of Strands

Equal thickness for each of the strands throughout their length, and equal twist are important. The thickness should not be greater than is necessary with the material being used. For grass rope, the strand should not be more than ¼-inch diameter, for coarse bark or palm not more than 1/8 or 3/16, for fine bark, hair or sisal fibre not more than 1/8 inch.

For cords the strand should be no more than one-sixteenth inch in diameter.

Fine cords cannot be made from grass, unless the fibres are separated by beating out and 'combing.'

The correct amount of twist is when the material is 'hard,' that is, the twist is tight.

Faults Common with Beginners

There is a tendency with the beginner to feed unevenly. Thin wispy sections of strand are followed by thick hunky portions. " Such feeding is useless. Rope made from such strands will break with less than one-quarter of the possible strain from the material.

The beginner is wise to twist and feed slowly, and to make regular, even strands rather than rush the job and try and make the strands quickly. Speed, with uniformity of twist and thickness, comes only with practice. In a short time when you have the 'feel' of feeding, you will find you can feed at the rate of from thirty to sixty feet a minute.

Thick strands do not help. It is useless to try and spin up a rope from strands an inch or more in thickness. Such a rope will break with less than half the potential strain of the material.

Spinning 'thick' strands does not save time in ropemaking.

Lianas, Vines and Canes

Lianas and ground vines are natural ropes, and grow in sub-tropical and tropical scrub and jungle. Many are of great strength, and useful for bridging, tree climbing and other purposes. The smaller ground vines when plaited give great strength and flexibility. Canes, and stalks of palms provide excellent material if used properly. Only the outer skin is tough and strong, and this skin will split off easily if you bend the main stalk away from the skin. This principle also applies to the splitting of lawyer cane (calamus), all the palm leaf stalks and all green material. If the split starts to run off, you must bend the material away from the thin side, and then it will gradually gain in size, and come back to an even thickness with the other split side.

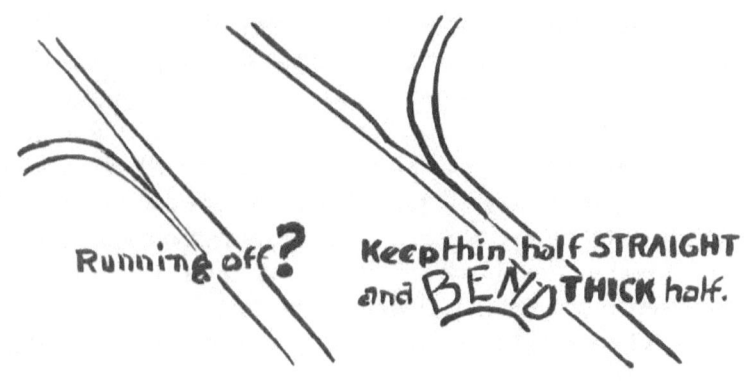

Running off? Keep thin half STRAIGHT and BEND THICK half.

Bark Fibres

The fibres in many barks which are suitable for rope making are close to the innermost layer. This is the bark next to the sap wood.

When seeking suitable barks of green timber, cut a small section about three inches long, and an inch wide. Cut this portion right from the wood to the outer skin of the bark.

Peel this specimen, and test the different layers. Green bark fibres are generally difficult to spin because of 'gum' and it is better to search around for windfallen dead branches and try the inner bark of these. The gum will probably have leached out, and the fibres separate very easily.

Many shrubs have excellent bark fibre, and here it is advisable to cut the end of a branch and peel off a strip of bark for testing. Thin barks from green shrubs are sometimes difficult to spin into fine cord and it is then easier to use the lariat plait for small cords.

Where it is necessary to use green bark fibre for rope spinning (if time permits), you will find that the gum will generally wash out when the bark is teased and soaked in water for a day or so.

After removing from the water; allow the bark strips to partly dry out before shredding and teasing into fibre.

Plaiting

One man may require a considerable length of rope, and if he has no assistance to help him spin up his material he can often find reasonably long material (say, from 1 ft. to 3 ft. or more) and using this material he can plait (or braid) and so make suitable rope. The usual three plait makes a flat rope, and while quite good, has not the finish or shape, nor is it as 'tight' as the four or lariat plait. On other occasions it may be necessary to plait broad bands for belts or for shoulder straps. There are many fancy braids and plaits which you can develop from these, but these three are basic, and essential for practical woodcraft work.

A general rule for all plaits is to work from the outside in to the centre.

Three Plait

Take the right-hand strand and pass it over the strand to the left.
Take the left-hand strand and pass it over the strand to the right and repeat alternately from left to right.

Flat Four Plait

Lay the four strands side by side. Take the right-hand strand as in Fig. 1 and lay it over the strand to the left.

Now take the outside *left-hand* strand as in Fig. 2 and lay it under the next strand to itself and over what was the first strand.

Take the outside left strand and put it under and over, the next two strands respectively moving towards the right.

Thereafter your right-hand strand goes over one strand to the left, and your lett-hand strand under and over to the right, as shown in Fig. 4.

Broad Plait

To commence. Take six, seven or more strands, and hold them flat and together.

Take a strand in the centre and pass it over the next strand to the left, as in Fig. 1.

Take the second strand in the centre to the left and pass it towards the right over the strand you first took so that it points towards the right as in Fig. 2.

Now take the next strand to the first one and weave it under and over as in Fig. 3.

Weave the next strands from left and right alternately towards the centre as in Fig. 4, 5, 6.

The finished plait should be tight and close as in Fig. 7.

To Finish Off

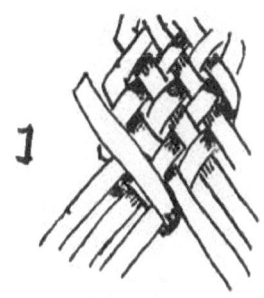

Take one of the centre strands, and lay it back upon itself as in Fig. 1.

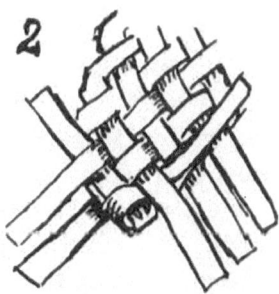

Now take the first strand which it enclosed in being folded back, and weave this back upon itself as in Fig. 2.

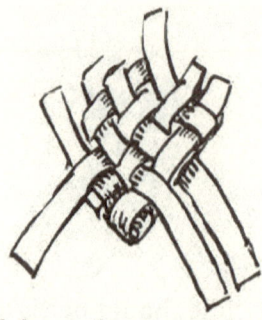

Take a strand from the opposite side, and lay it back and weave it between the strands already plaited.

All the strands should be so woven back that no strands show an uneven pattern, and there should be a regular under-over-under of the alternating weaves.

If you have plaited tightly there may be a difficulty in working the loose ends between the plaited strands.

This can be done easily if you sharpen a thin piece of wood to a chisel edge, and use this to open the strands sufficiently to allow the ends being finished to pass between the woven strands.

Roll under a bottle to work smooth after finishing off.

Round or Lariat Plait... Four Strands

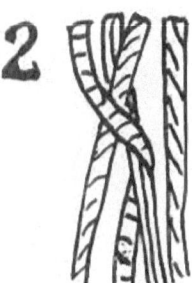

1. Lay the four strands together side by side, as in Fig. 1, and cross the right-hand centre strand over, and then around the left-hand strand.

2. Take the left-hand outside strand, and pass it over the two crossed strands, and then under the right-hand one of the two, so that it is pointing towards the left, as in Fig. 2.

3. Take the free right-hand strand, and pass it over the two twisted strands to the left and completely round the left-hand one of the two, as in Fig. 3.

4. Repeat this with the outside left-hand strand as in Fig. 4.

5. Repeat with the right-hand strand as in Fig. 5.

6. The finished plait should look like this.

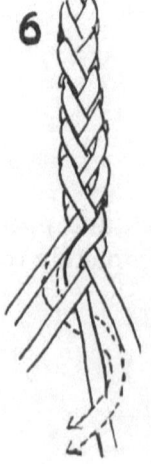

Climbing with Footlock

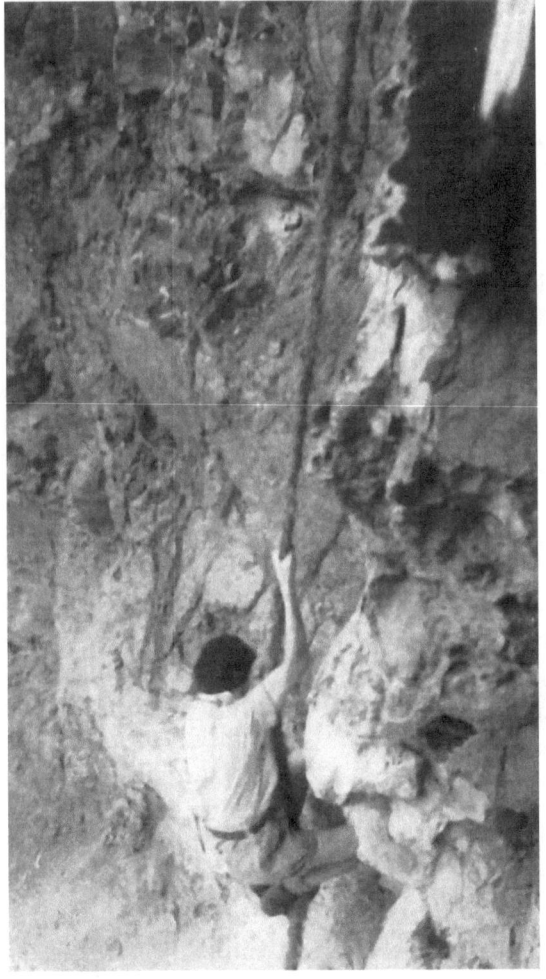

Ascent of a cliff face, using a footlock on a grass rope. The grass rope was 3 strand 3 lay of 2 inches diameter.

CAUTION: Prior to trusting your life to a bush-made rope, always test it. Tie one end to a tree and put three or four fellows onto the other end. Have them take the strain gently until finally all their weight is on the rope. If they cannot break it, then it is safe for one man at a time to use it to climb or descend a cliff face.

When climbing up a bush-made rope always use the footlock, and when descending never slide down the rope. *Climb* down again using the same footlock.

The footlock offers a measure of safety, and the climber is so secure that he can actually stand on the rope and rest without his body weight being carried entirely on his arms. To prove this, use the footlock, and clasp the rope to your body with your arms. You will find that you are 'standing' on the rope and quite secure.

By means of the footlock you can climb to any height on the rope, stopping to rest when your arms tire.

The footlock is made by holding onto the rope with both hands, lifting the knees, and kicking the rope to the outside of one foot. The foot on the opposite side to the rope is 'pointed' so that the toe picks up the rope, which is pulled over the foot which was against the rope, and under the instep of the foot which 'picked' it up.

The two feet are brought together, and the rope is now over the instep of one foot, and under the ball of the other. Then, to secure the grip, and lock the rope; the feet are placed one on top of the other so that the rope is clamped down by the foot on top.

By straightening the knees, and raising the hands, the body is lifted, and a fresh grip taken for the next rise.

In descending, the body is bent, the hands lowered, and the footlock released, and a fresh grip taken with the feet at a lower level on the rope.

It is advisable to wear boots or shoes when climbing bush-made ropes.

This method of descending is much safer than sliding. In sliding there is grave risk of bad rope burns to hands and legs.

'Absyle' for Rock Descent

Photo with acknowledgment to "S.M. Herald"

Absyle used for descending rock face. This bush-made grass rope is 3 strand 3 lay of about 2 inches diameter. Breaking strain approx. 400 lbs.

The 'Absyle' is used for rock work, generally for descending, though it can be used on some faces for ascent.

In the 'Absyle' the body is upright, but the legs are stretched out, and the feet pressed against the rock face.

The rope passes down between the thighs, around one thigh and diagonally up and across the upper half of the body and over the shoulder opposite to the leg under which it passes. The rope may be gripped with one hand.

In descending, the free hand pulls the rope over the shoulder. This leaves a loop below the thigh, and the feet are walking' down the rock face until the thigh is again impossible to fall.

In ascending a rock face which has an extreme slope but is not vertical, the feet are 'walked' up the rock face, the body is pulled up the rope, and the slack, hanging below the legs, is pulled up with one hand and fed over the shoulder. By this means the climber can 'sit' on the rope and rest. When using the 'Absyle' it will be found that bare feet, sandshoes or spiked shoes give a better grip on the rock face than plain leather soles.

Tying Split Canes and Vines Together

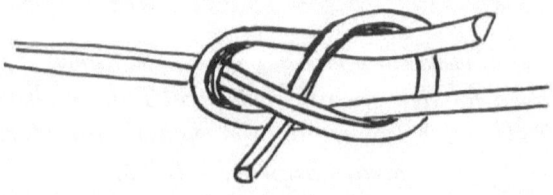

These materials will only tie with special knots and it is a safe rule to tie with the outside of the skin on the outside bend of the knot, as in A. If you try to tie with the inside of the material on the outer surface of the bend (as in B), it is probable that the material will either crack or snap off, and you may reject it as useless. The knots which are most suitable for tying these canes and vines are:

Joining knots: Sheet bend, Reef knot, and fisherman
Securing knots: Timber hitch.

When pulling the knot taut, do so gently. If you snap
the joining knot the material may either cut itself or break.
If the canes or vines are brittle through greenness try heat
treatment.

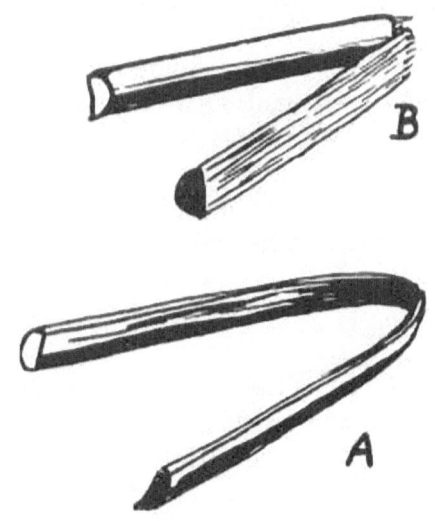

Uses for Bush-Made Ropes

There are many occasions when bush-made ropes can
be extremely useful ... for climbing or descending a short cliff
face; for climbing a tree; for a rope bridge; for a safety-line
across a fast or flooded river.

Single Rope Ladder with Sticks

A single rope ladder is made by opening the
lays of the rope and inserting cross sticks each about 8 inches
long as shown with an equal amount protruding on either
side of the rope. These cross sticks must be secured to the
rope, and it is necessary to lash the rope above and below the
sticks. The distance between the sticks should be from 15" to
18".

To climb a rope ladder, hold the rope with both hands, bend the knees, and draw both feet up together and lay them with even pressure on the next cross sticks. When the footing is secure, raise the hands and continue the action, which is somewhat like that of a toy monkey on a string.

Bush single-rope ladders have the advantage that they can be used easily by people who may not be able to climb by ordinary means. They provide an easy means of ascending and descending a cliff or a lookout.

Single Rope Ladder with Chocks

This type of ladder has the advantage of being portable and quickly made. The chocks of hardwood are about 6" diameter and 2" deep, and are suitably bored to take the diameter of the rope. Splice an eye at the top end and seize in a thimble to lash the rope head securely. To secure the chocks, put two strands of seizing between the strands of the rope and then work a wall knot.

Rope Bridge

Two ropes are spun. They must be very strong and thoroughly tested. They are anchored to either side of the river, either to convenient trees or to anchors as shown.

When these ropes have been stretched taut, light 'A' frames are made. The number required depends upon the length of the decking.

The first 'A' frame is hooked onto the ropes and pushed forward with a stick. The footing, a straight sapling, is dropped down onto the crotch of the frame, and the bridge builder walks out along this and hooks on the next 'A' frame, pushing it out the required distance, and repeats the process till the far bank is reached. Rope bridges must not be overloaded—one at a time is a safe rule. If Monkey vines,

Lianas, or Lawyer vines (Calamus) are available instead of bush-made rope, use any of these. They are much stronger and will make a bridge strong enough for 4 to 6 men at a time.

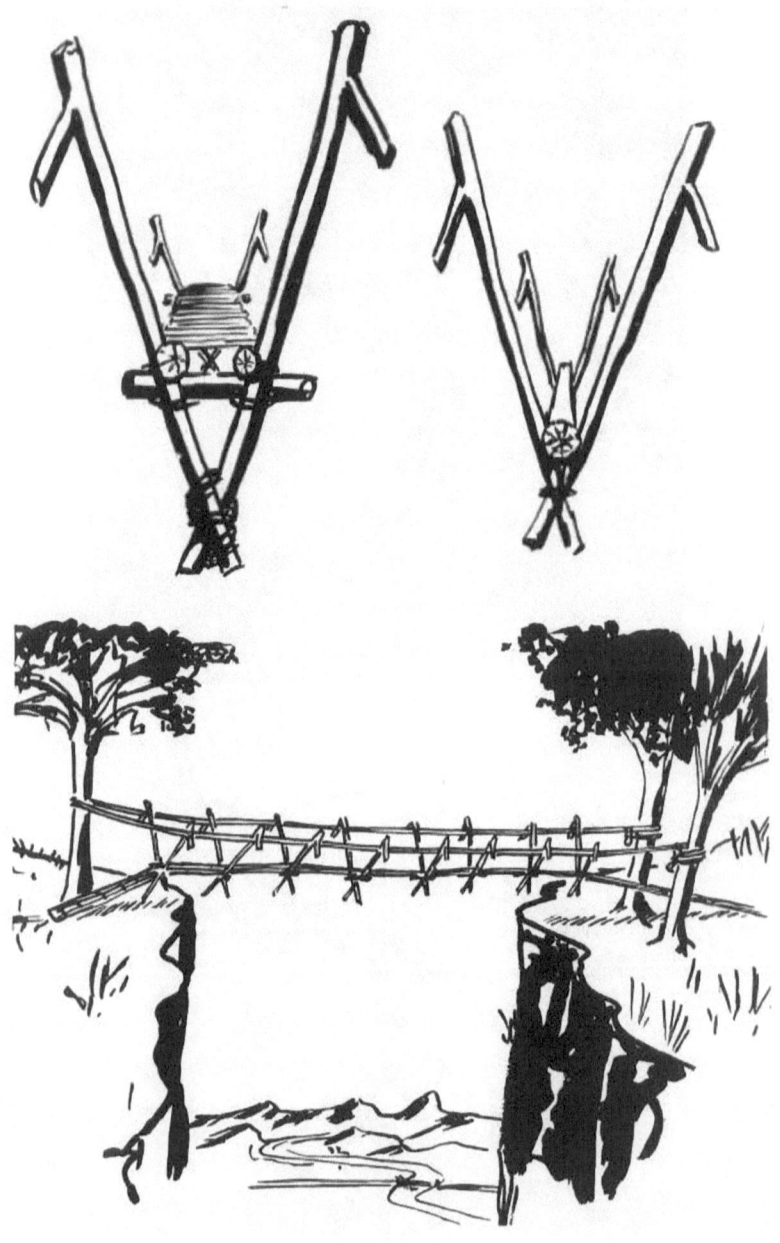

To Measure the Distance Across a River or Gorge

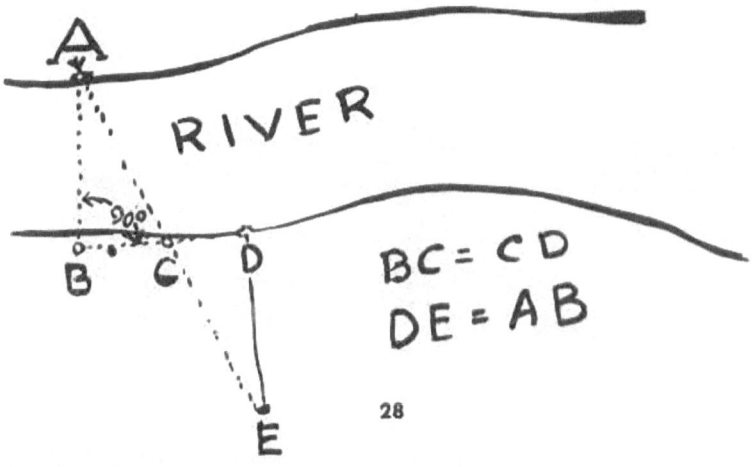

$$BC = CD$$
$$DE = AB$$

28

Select a mark on the opposite bank 'A,' and then drive a stake on the near bank 'B.' Walk at right angles for a known number of paces and put in another marker stake 'C,' and continue an equal number of paces and put in a third marker 'D.'

Turn at right angles away from the river, and keep moving back until the centre marker stake and the mark on the other side of the river are in line 'E.'

Measure the distance from the third or last marker peg 'D' to this point 'E,' and this distance will equal the distance across the river.

To Get a Rope Across a Narrow, Deep River

Fasten a stout stick to the end of the rope. The rope must be in the middle of the stick. Select a forked tree on the opposite bank. Throw the free end of the coiled line with the stick across the river to the tree. After many casts when it has caught, test with two or three people to make sure the line is secure. Fasten the near end of the rope to a convenient anchor, and then the person crossing the line (usually the lightest member of the party) hangs onto the line, lifts his legs and hooks them over the rope, with his feet towards the opposite bank. By this means he can work himself across the river, fasten the rope, and do all the work which has to be done on that side of the river.

31

Safety Line for River Crossing

A bush rope can be spun to serve as a safety line for crossing flooded or fast rivers. The rope is taken across by one member of the party, and fastened to an anchor on the opposite bank. As a safety line it should be above water level. The person crossing should stand on the downstream side of the rope, and face upstream. He crosses by moving his feet sideways, one step at a time, and holding all the time to the rope which helps him keep his balance. If by chance the current is so strong that it sweeps him off his feet, his grip on the line will save him from being washed downstream, and he can work his way shoreward hand over hand, until he is a less strong portion of the current where he can regain his footing.

1-2-3 Anchor

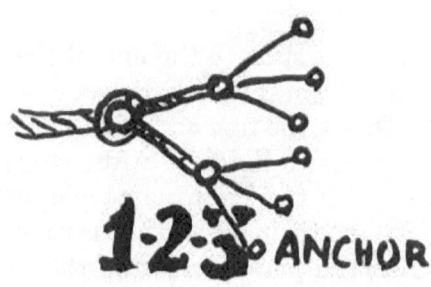

A very stout stake is driven into the ground, at an angle of about 45°, and to the foot of this the main rope to be anchored is fastened. To the head of this stake two ropes are secured and these are fastened to the foot of two stakes to the rear. The heads of these stakes are in turn tied back to the foot of three other stakes. This anchor will hold secure under almost all conditions.

Anchoring a Peg in Sand

The only way to anchor a rope into soft sand is to attach it to a peg, and bury the peg in the sand.

Scrape a trench in the sand to a depth of between a foot and eighteen inches, deeper if high winds or very stormy weather are expected. Pass the rope round the centre of the peg; scratch a channel for it at right angles to the pegtrench.

Fill in the trench and rope channel, and fasten the free end of the rope to the standing end with a stopper hitch, and pull taut. The buried peg should hold a tent rope in sand under all normal weather conditions.

Bush Windlass

A bush windlass, capable of taking a very heavy strain on a rope can be made by selecting a site where a tree forks low to the ground, with the fork facing the direction in which the pull is required. Alternatively, a stout fork can be driven in and anchored with the "1-2-3" method.

The windlass portion is a forked log. The forks are notched to take the lever (up to seven feet long). The rope is passed round the roller a few times so that it locks upon itself. (If the fork of the roller is long, the rope may pass through the fork.)

This type of bush windlass has many uses.

www.ingramcontent.com/pod-product-compliance
Lightning Source LLC
Chambersburg PA
CBHW050524290526
45786CB00007B/2689